Eduard Mörike

Hugo Wolf

THE COMPLETE MÖRIKE SONGS

With a New Prose Translation of the Texts by
STANLEY APPELBAUM

DOVER PUBLICATIONS, INC.
NEW YORK

Published in Canada by General Publishing Company, Ltd., 30 Lesmill Road, Don Mills, Toronto, Ontario.
Published in the United Kingdom by Constable and Company, Ltd.

This Dover edition, first published in 1982, is an unabridged republication of the second revised edition of *Gedichte von Eduard Mörike für eine Singstimme und Klavier componirt (1888) von Hugo Wolf*, as published by K. Ferd. Heckel in Mannheim, n.d.
The translations, as well as the preliminary lists and glossary, were prepared specially for the present edition by Stanley Appelbaum.

International Standard Book Number: 0-486-24380-X

Manufactured in the United States of America
Dover Publications, Inc., 180 Varick Street, New York, N.Y. 10014

Contents

Alphabetical List of Song Titles

Alphabetical List of Song Openings

Glossary of German Terms
Occurring on the Music Pages

To avoid extensive repetition, some of the phrases have been broken down into their component words; for instance, *mässig langsam* ("moderately slowly") will be found by com-bining *mässig* ("moderately") and *langsam* ("slowly"), both of which words may enter into other combinations.

abnehmend: diminuendo
allmählig: gradually
anschwellend: swelling, getting louder
arpeggiren: to play as an arpeggio
ausdrucksvoll: with expression; espressivo
äusserst: extremely
bedeutend: significantly
belebt(er): in a (more) lively manner
beschleunigend(er): accelerating (more)
beschleunigter: with greater acceleration
bewegt(er): (more) agitatedly; (più) mosso
breit: broadly; largamente
das Motiv im Basse markirt: the motif in the bass marcato
dieselbe Bewegung: at the same pace
diskret mauschelnd: with a slight Jewish accent*
drängend: with urgency; stringendo
durchweg: throughout
eilen: to hurry
einfach: with simplicity; semplice
ein wenig: a little; un poco
energisch: energetically
entschlossen: with resolve; risoluto
erregt(er): more excitedly; (più) eccitato
ersterbend: dying away; morendo
erstes (or:1^{s}; I.) Zeitmass: original tempo; tempo primo
etwas: somewhat
feierlich: solemnly; solenne
feierliches Marschtempo: solemn march tempo
feurig: with fire; con fuoco
flüsternd: whispering
frisch: briskly
fromm: piously
gedehnt: drawn out, sustained
gehalten: sustained; sostenuto
geheimnissvoll: mysteriously; misterioso
gemächlich: at a comfortable pace

*This anti-Semitism is Wolf's, not Mörike's. The song has been successfully performed without the Jewish accent.

gemessen: steadily, deliberately
Gesang: voice
gesteigerter: with greater intensity
getragen: sustained, smoothly
gewichtig: weightily; pesante
gleiche Bewegung: at the same pace
glühend: ardently
graziös: gracefully; grazioso
gut gehalten: well sustained; ben sostenuto
heftig: violently
hingebend: enthusiastically
im Hauptzeitmasse: at the principal tempo
im Marschtempo: at a march tempo
immer: always, throughout, more and more (sempre più; as in *immer erregter:* more and more excitedly)
im (Tempo und) Vortrag gesteigert: heightened in (tempo and) delivery
innig: fervently
jubelnd: jubilantly
keck: jauntily
kräftig: forcefully; con forza
kurz: short
lang(e): long
langsam(er): (more) slowly
lebhaft(er): (more) vivaciously; (più) vivace
leicht: lightly
leidenschaftlich(er): more passionately; (più) appassionato
leise(r): (more) quietly
luftig: airily
lustig: merrily
mässig: moderately; moderato
mehr: more
mit freiem Vortrag: declaiming freely
mit gesteigertem Ausdruck: with heightened expressiveness
mit hohler, heiserer Stimme: in a hollow, hoarse voice
mit Humor: humorously
mit innigster (OR: der innigsten) Empfindung: with the most fervent feeling
munter: cheerily

nachlassend: slackening
nach und nach: gradually, little by little
noch langsamer: still more slowly
nicht: not, do not
nicht zu: not too
Pause: rest, pause
phantastisch: with fantasy, fancifully
pompös: pompously
rasch: swiftly
ruhig(er): (more) calmly; (più) tranquillo
schleichend: creeping, stealthily
schmerzlich: sorrowfully
schnell(er): (more) quickly
schwebend: floating, soaring
schwer: heavily, with difficulty
schwermüthig: with melancholy
sehr: very
sehr mässiges Walzertempo: very moderate waltz tempo
sehr ruhige Bewegung: at a very calm pace
sich verlierend: disappearing; perdendosi
stark: strongly
trübe: gloomily
überströmend: overflowing
und (u.): and
verdrossen: with vexation
verklingend: dying away
Verschiebung: soft pedal
weich: softly, sweetly
weihevoll: solemnly, religiously
wieder: again
wie ein Hauch: like a puff of air
wie im Traum: as if dreaming
wie in tiefes Sinnen verloren: as if lost in deep thought
wie zu Anfang: as at the beginning
wild: wildly
zart: gently, tenderly
ziemlich: rather, fairly
zitternd: trembling
zögernd: hesitating
zunehmend: crescendo
zurückhaltend: holding back

Translations

All the original texts are by the German poet Eduard Mörike (1804–1875). The songs were all composed in 1888 and originally published in Vienna in 1889. In the present volume the singing translations of the songs "Verborgenheit," "Der Gärtner," "Gebet" and "Gesang Weyla's" that appeared in the edition being reproduced have been retained under the music in addition to the literal prose translations included in this section.

1. *Der Genesene an die Hoffnung* (Address to Hope by a Man Recovered from Illness)

Day was dawning fatally for me, but my head already lay sheltered, oh so sweetly, in your lap, O Hope, until the victory was won, until the victory was won. I made sacrifices to all the gods, but you were forgotten; placed apart from the eternal saviors, you observed the feast. Oh, forgive me, you most loyal one! Step out of your twilight and let me take a look at your eternally new, moon-bright face; let me take a hearty look, like a child and free from grief. Ah, just once enfold me in your arms without pain!

2. *Der Knabe und das Immlein* (The Boy and the Bee)

In the vineyard on the hill a little house stands so fearful of the wind; it has neither door nor window, and it suffers from boredom. And when the day is very sultry and all the songbirds have fallen silent, a bee buzzes around the sunflower all alone. "My darling has a garden; in it stands a pretty beehive: have you come flying from there? Has she sent you out after me?" Oh, no, you fine lad, no one told me to deliver messages. That girl knows nothing about love; she has barely looked at you yet. What do you expect girls to know when they are hardly out of school! Your beloved sweetheart is still her mother's little baby. I am bringing her wax and honey; goodbye! I have a whole pound. How the little darling will laugh; her mouth is already watering. Ah, if you wanted to tell her, I know something that's much sweeter: there is nothing lovelier on earth than hugging and kissing! nothing lovelier on earth than hugging and kissing!"

3. *Ein Stündlein wohl vor Tag* (About an Hour Before Daybreak)

While I lay sleeping, about an hour before daybreak, a little swallow sang to me from the tree in front of my window; I barely heard it, about an hour before daybreak: "Listen to what I tell you. I bring an accusation against your sweetheart: at the very moment I am singing this, he is hugging another girl, as carefree as he can be, about an hour before daybreak." "Oh, woe, speak no further! Be quiet! I don't want to hear anything! Fly away, fly away from my tree! Ah, love and fidelity are like a dream, about an hour before daybreak."

4. *Jägerlied* (Hunter's Song)

Dainty is the bird's footprints in the snow when it walks on the mountain heights: my darling's dear hand writes more daintily, writes a letter to me in far-off lands. A heron rises high into the sky, so high that neither arrow nor bullet can reach it: a thousand times as high and rapid are the thoughts of true lovers.

5. *Der Tambour* (The Drummer Boy)

If my mother could work magic, she would have to travel with the regiment, to France, everywhere, and she would be the canteen keeper. In the camp, about midnight, when no one is up except the sentries, and everyone is snoring, both horses and men, then I would sit down in front of my drum: the drum would be changed into a bowl with hot sauerkraut in it, the drumsticks would become a knife and fork, my saber would become a long sausage, my shako would be a good tankard that I would fill with burgundy. And because I

need light, the moon shines into my tent. Even if it shines in in French, I still start thinking about my sweetheart: oh, woe! oh, woe! oh, woe! woe! Now the fun is over! If my mother could only work magic! If my mother could work magic!

6. *Er ist's* (It Is He)

Springtime lets its blue ribbon flutter through the sky again; sweet, familiar fragrances brush against the land like a premonition. Violets are already dreaming; they will soon be here. Listen! from afar, the soft note of a harp! Springtime, yes, it's you! Springtime, yes, it's you! I have heard you! Yes, it's you!

7. *Das verlassene Mägdlein* (The Forsaken Servant Girl)

Early, when the roosters crow, before the stars disappear, I must stand at the hearth, I must light the fire. Beautiful is the glow of the flames, the sparks leap; I stare into the fire, sunk in sorrow. Suddenly I remember, faithless boy, that last night I dreamed about you. Tear after tear then flows down my cheeks. That is how the day begins — oh, I wish it were over!

8. *Begegnung* (Meeting)

What a storm there was last night until morning finally stirred itself! How the broom, without our asking, swept out the chimney and the alleys! Here comes a girl already walking in the street, looking all around half-scared; the color in her little face comes and goes, like roses that the wind has blown apart. A handsome young man walks toward her; full of happiness, he wants to approach her: how joyfully and bashfully the inexperienced rascals look at each other! He seems to ask whether his sweetheart has already rearranged her braids that a storm disordered last night in the open room. The young man is still dreaming of the kisses that the sweet girl exchanged with him; he stands, enraptured by her grace, while she dashes around the corner.

9. *Nimmersatte Liebe* (Insatiable Love)

That's how love is! That's how love is! It can't be quenched with kisses. What fool would try to fill a sieve with nothing but water? Even if you ladle for a thousand years — if you kiss eternally, even eternally — you will never satisfy love. Love, love has amazing new appetites all the time. We bit each other's lips till they bled when we kissed today. The girl stood there patiently, like a lamb under the knife. Her eyes asked: "Please keep on; the more it hurts, the better I like it!" That's how love is, and that's how it has been as long as love has existed; and when Solomon the Wise was in love, he was no different; and when Solomon the Wise was in love, he was no different.

10. *Fussreise* (Journey on Foot)

When, leaning on my freshly cut hiking stick, I wander like this in the morning through forests, up and down hills, then — as the songbird sings and hops about in the leaves, or as the golden grapes perceive spirits of bliss in the first rays of the morning sun — thus also my inmost nature, the dear old Adam within me, feels an autumn and springtime fever, the pristine bliss of Paradise, a bliss that is confident in God and was never lost through folly. And so, old Adam, you are not as bad as the severe theologians say. You still love and praise after all, you still sing and glorify your beloved Creator and Preserver as if you were living ever-new days of Creation. If He so grants, my entire life would be such a morning journey as this, with the light perspiration of the wanderer on my brow!

11. *An eine Aeolsharfe* (To an Aeolian Harp)

[The Latin quotation from Horace: You constantly dwell on the loss of Mystes in weeping tones; your love gives you no respite either when the evening star rises or when it flees the rapid approach of the sun.]

Leaning against the ivy-clad wall of this old terrace, you, the mysterious stringed instrument of an air-born muse, begin, once more begin your melodious plaint! You come here, O winds, from afar, ah, from the fresh green of the hill where dwells the boy who was so dear to me. And brushing against spring blossoms on your way, saturated with fragrances, how sweetly, how sweetly, how sweetly you oppress my heart! How sweetly you oppress my heart! And you rustle here into the strings, drawn by euphonious melancholy, swelling in the draft of my yearning, and dying away again. But all at once, as the wind pushes this way more violently, a lovely cry of the harp—to my sweet alarm—repeats the sudden stirring of my soul; and here the full-blown rose, shaken, strews all its petals at my feet!

12. *Verborgenheit* (Seclusion)

Let, O world, oh, let me be! Do not lure me with the gifts of love. Let my heart possess alone its bliss, its pain! What I sorrow over, I do not know; it is unfamiliar grief. It is always through tears that I see the sun's dear light. Often I am barely conscious of myself, and bright joy cuts through the heaviness that weighs upon me and kindles rapture in my breast. Let, O world, oh, let me be! Do not lure me with the gifts of love. Let my heart possess alone its bliss, its pain!

13. *Im Frühling* (In Springtime)

Here I lie on the springtime hill: the cloud becomes my wings, a bird flies out ahead of me. Ah, tell me, my one and only love, where you are, so that I can be with you! But you and the sky have no dwelling place. My spirit is wide open like the sunflower, yearning, expanding, in love and hope. Springtime, what is your will? When will I be satisfied? I see the cloud and the river pass by; the sun's golden kiss penetrates deep within me. My eyes, in a wondrous stupor, seem to be dropping off to sleep; only my ears are still active, listening to the music of the bee. I think about this and that; I feel a longing but don't exactly know what for: it's half pleasure and half lament. My heart, tell me, what recollections are you weaving in the twilight of the golden-green branches? Old, unnamable days!

14. *Agnes*

Season of roses! how quickly you went by, how quickly by! If my lover had remained true, remained true, I would not be afraid. As they cut the grain, the harvest women sing happily, happily. But alas, my spirit is sick, my spirit is sick, and nothing goes right for me. Thus I slink through the valley meadows, through the valley, as if lost in a dream, and I go to the mountain where a thousand times, a thousand times he swore to me that he would be true. Up there at the edge of the hill, turning aside, I weep by the lime tree. On my hat, the band of roses, which he made, plays in the wind.

15. *Auf einer Wanderung* (On a Foot Journey)

I enter a friendly little town; red glow of evening is in the streets. Just at that moment, from an open window, across the richest display of flowers, golden bell tones are heard floating in the air, and a voice that sounds like a choir of nightingales, so that the blossoms tremble, the sky comes to life and the roses gleam forth in heightened redness. For a long time I stood still in amazement, aching with happiness. I really don't know, myself, how I got outside the town gate. Ah, how bright the world is here! The sky surges in a purple tumult; behind me is the town in a golden haze. How the alder-lined brook murmurs, how the mill in the valley clatters! I feel as if intoxicated, led astray—O Muse, you have touched my heart with a breath of love!

16. *Elfenlied* (Elf Song)

At night in the village the watchman called: "Eleven o'clock!" [*Elfe*, which also means "elf"]. A very small elf was sleeping in the forest about eleven o'clock! And thought that the nightingale was calling him by name from the valley, or that Silpelit* had called to him. The elf rubbed his eyes, went to his snail shell and acted like a drunken

---

*In some of his fanciful pieces, Mörike developed his own imaginary characters; another example occurring in the Wolf songs is Weyla.

---

man because he hadn't slept himself out. So he stumbled, tip tap, through the hazel thicket down into the valley, and glided along the town wall, keeping quite close to it. There sat the glowworms, light by light. "What are those little bright windows? There's probably a wedding going on inside: the little folk are seated at their meal and making merry in the great hall. I'll just take a peek in." Ouch! he banged his head against hard stone! Elf, tell me, have you had enough? Cuckoo! Elf, tell me, have you had enough? Cuckoo! Cuckoo! Cuckoo! Cuckoo!

17. *Der Gärtner* (The Gardener)

On her favorite horse, as white as the snow, the loveliest princess rides down the tree-lined avenue. On the path, along which her steed prances so gracefully, the sand that I sprinkled glistens like gold. You rose-colored cap bobbing up and down, oh, secretly drop a feather for me! And if you want a flower from me in exchange, take a thousand for one, take all of them for it! Take a thousand for one, take all of them for it!

18. *Citronenfalter im April* (Brimstone Butterfly in April)

Cruel springtime sun, you awaken me prematurely. The delicate food I live on grows only in the bliss of May! If there is no dear girl here who will offer me a drop of honey on her rosy lips, then I must perish in misery, and May will never behold me in my yellow attire, in my yellow attire.

19. *Um Mitternacht* (Around Midnight)

Calmly Night descended upon the land, and now leans dreaming against the wall of the mountains. Her eyes now see the golden balance of time in the perfect repose of equal scales. And the springs bubble forth more jauntily; they sing in the ear of Mother Night about the day, about the day that has just passed. The old, the age-old slumber song—she pays no heed to it, she is tired of it. Sweeter yet to her is the sound of the blue sky, and the evenly borne yoke of the swift-moving hours. But the springs still continue their message. Even in sleep the waters go on singing about the day, about the day that has just passed.

20. *Auf eine Christblume. I* (On a Christmas Rose, I)

You daughter of the forest, kindred to the lily, sought so long by me, unknown—in a strange churchyard, bleak and wintry, for the first time, beautiful one, I find you! Tended by whose hand you blossomed here, I do not know, nor whose grave you guard. If it is a young man's, then he found salvation; if it is a maiden's, her lot was an enviable one. In the nocturnal grove, covered over with snowy light, where the deer piously passes you as it grazes, near the chapel, by the crystal pool, there I sought the magical realm of your homeland. You are beautiful, child of the moon—not of the sun. The rapture of other flowers would be fatal to you; the balmily sweet air of heaven's chill nourishes you and your chaste body full of hoarfrost and fragrance. Deep within the golden abundance of your bosom is a perfume that makes itself known only imperceptibly. The same fragrance emanated from the bridal dress of the Blessed Mother, touched by an angel's hand. Five purple drops, a reminder of the Holy Passion, would be perfectly and uniquely becoming to you: but, childlike, in the Christmas season you adorn your white gown with a breath of delicate green. The elf that goes to join the dance in the moonlit valley at the midnight hour, stands still at a distance in shy curiosity at the sight of your mystic glory, and then darts past.

21. *Auf eine Christblume. II* (On a Christmas Rose, II)

In the wintry earth sleeps—a flower seed—the butterfly, which will flutter on its velvet wings around bush and hill on spring nights. It will never taste your sweet nectar. But who knows whether its tender spirit, when all the beauties of summer have passed away, may not at some time—intoxicated by your gentle fragrance, and unseen by me—circle around your blossoms?

22. *Seufzer. Crux fidelis* (Sigh. Faithful Cross)

[The Latin quotation from Fortunatus' hymn on the Passion: Kind Jesus, in Whose flame I wish to burn, in love for You, why have I not burned? Why have I not loved You, Jesus Christ? Oh, how sad is this coldness!]

The flame of Your love, O Lord, how dearly I would foster it, tend it! I have not fostered it, have not tended it. I am dead in my heart — oh, pains of Hell!

23. *Auf ein altes Bild* (On an Old Painting)

In the summery haze of a green landscape, by cool water, sedges and reeds, see how the Child in innocent freedom plays while seated in the Virgin's lap! And there in the blissful forest, alas, the Cross tree is already in green leaf!

24. *In der Frühe* (Early in the Morning)

No sleep has yet refreshed my eyes, and day is already appearing at my bedroom window. My disordered mind is still groping among doubts, and creating nocturnal specters. Feel no more alarm, cease torturing yourself, my soul! Rejoice! Here and there morning bells have already awakened.

25. *Schlafendes Jesuskind. Gemalt von Franc. Albani* (Sleeping Christ Child. Painting by Francesco Albani)

Son of the Virgin, heavenly child! You have fallen asleep on the ground on the wooden beam of Your sorrows, which the pious artist, with symbolic fancy, placed beneath You as a pillow for Your weightless dreams. You are a flower, and the glory of Your Father is still faintly enclosed in the bud! Oh, if we could only see what images are painted in soft alternation behind that brow, behind those dark lashes! Son of the Virgin, heavenly Child.

26. *Charwoche* (Passion Week)

O week that witnessed holy suffering! You sound such a serious note in this blissful spring season; in the rejuvenated rays of the sun you spread the shadow of the Cross over the bright earth, and silently lower your mourning crape. Meanwhile, the spring is allowed to go on germinating; the violet is fragrant beneath blossoming trees and all the birds sing songs of joy. Oh, be silent, you birds in the green meadows! All around, hollow-toned bells are sounding; the angels are softly singing dirges. Oh, quiet, you birds high up in the blue sky! You violets, do not crown any maiden's tresses today! My pious girl is picking you to make a dark bouquet; you will accompany her to the Virgin Mary's house, and there you will wither on the altar of the Lord. Ah, there, intoxicated by mournful melodies and sweetly dazed by heavy fumes of incense, she seeks her bridegroom in the vaults of death, and love and springtime —everything is lost!

27. *Zum neuen Jahr. Kirchengesang* (For the New Year. Hymn)

Just as an angel, in mysterious manner, softly walks upon the earth with rosy feet, thus did morning approach. Joyfully give it a holy welcome, all you faithful! My heart, you too rejoice! Let our beginning be in Him Who moves moons and suns in the blue tabernacles of heaven. You, Father, give counsel! Guide us and direct us! Lord, may beginning and end, may everything, everything, be placed in Your hands!

28. *Gebet* (Prayer)

Lord! send me what You will, something dear or something painful. I am satisfied that both emanate from Your hands. Do not overwhelm me with joys or with sorrows! But in the middle, but in the middle lies gracious moderation.

29. *An den Schlaf* (To Sleep)

[The Latin quotation from Meibom: Light sleep, although you are the very image of death, I nevertheless desire you to share my bed. Healthful repose, so ardently wished for, come! For how sweet it is to live like this without life, to die like this without death!]

Sleep, sweet sleep! Although nothing resembles death as much as you do, nevertheless I welcome you to this bed! For devoid of life, like this, how lovely it is to live! So far from dying, ah, how easy it is to die!

30. *Neue Liebe* (New Love)

Can a human being on this earth really belong completely to another, as much as he may wish to? Through the long night I thought about this, and had to answer no! Thus, can I not be called anyone's on this earth, and can no one be mine? Out of the darkness a ray of joy flashed brightly within me: may I not be in a mine-and-yours relationship with God, as I wish to be? What can keep me from being so today? A pleasurable panic traverses my inmost being! I marvel that I considered it an impossible marvel to possess God as my own here on earth!

31. *Wo find' ich Trost* (Where Can I Find Solace?)

I know a love that is true, that has been loyal ever since I came upon it, that has bound itself to me with deep sighs ever afresh, constantly forgiving. It is He Who once bitterly drank the bitter drop of death with heavenly patience, Who hung on the Cross and atoned for my faults until they were submerged in a sea of grace. And why is it that I am sad now, that I writhe on the floor in anguish? I ask: "Watchman, will the night soon be over?" and: "What will save me from death and sin?" Wicked heart! why not confess: you have once again conceived an evil desire; the track of pious love, of pious fidelity, alas — it has now perished, and for a long time to come. Yes, that is why I am sad, why I writhe on the floor in anguish. Watchman, watchman, will the night soon be over? And what will save me from death and sin?

32. *An die Geliebte* (To the Beloved Woman)

When my need to gaze upon you has been thoroughly gratified and I take silent pleasure in your saintly virtues, then I hear plainly the soft breathing of the angel that is hidden within you. And a marveling, questioning smile plays upon my lips: is a dream deceiving me if I now believe that my boldest wish, my only wish, is fulfilled in you in eternally full measure? Then my mind plummets from depth to greater depth; from the nocturnal distance of the Godhead I hear the melodious sound of the fountains of destiny. In a stupor, I direct my gaze upward to the sky. There all the stars are smiling. I kneel to listen to their song of light.

33. *Peregrina. Aus: Maler Nolten. I* (Peregrina, excerpt from the novel *Nolten the Painter*, I)

The mirror of your faithful brown eyes is like a reflection of the gold within. They seem to absorb the gold from deep within your bosom, where it probably flourishes in sacred affliction. To plunge into that night of your gaze, innocent girl, you yourself invite me. You want me rashly to inflame myself and you. Smiling, you hand me death in the goblet of sin!

34. *Peregrina. II*

Why, beloved, do I think of you all at once now and shed a thousand tears, and can find no contentment, and why does my heart swell to bursting? Ah, yesterday, you portrait of sorrow beautified by sympathy, you entered the bright nursery by the flickering light of ornately arranged tapers and found me enjoying forgetfulness in bustle and games. It was your ghost; it sat down to the meal. We sat like strangers with silently suppressed sorrows. Finally I burst into loud sobbing, and hand in hand we left the house.

35. *Frage und Antwort* (Question and Answer)

Do you ask me how this timorous love came into my heart and why I have not long since removed its bitter sting? Tell my why the wind beats its wings with the swiftness of spirits, and where the sweet fountain receives its hidden waters. Stop the wind as it travels at full speed! With your magic wand, forbid the sweet fountains to flow!

36. *Lebe wohl* (Farewell)

"Farewell" — you do not feel what that word of sorrow means. You had a courageous expression and light heart when you said it. Farewell! Ah, I have repeated it to myself a thousand times, and when I did, I broke my heart with insatiable anguish!

37. *Heimweh* (Homesickness)

With every step that takes me farther away from my darling, the world becomes different. My heart refuses to come along any further. Here the sunshine falls coldly on the earth; here everything seems unfamiliar to me, even the flowers by the brook! Every object has such a strange expression, such a false appearance. It's true that the brook murmurs and says: "Poor boy, come over to me. Here too you will see forget-me-nots." Yes, they are beautiful wherever they grow, but not as beautiful as they were back there. Onward, keep moving onward! My eyes are full of tears!

38. *Lied vom Winde* (Song of the Wind)

Rustling wind, raging wind, now here, now there! Rustling wind, raging wind, tell me, where is your homeland? "My child, we have been roaming for many, many years through the wide, wide world, and we would like to find that out, to hunt down the answer. We have asked the mountains, the oceans, the resounding hosts of heaven, and none of them knows, and none of them knows, and none of them knows. If you are cleverer than they, you can tell us. Let's go! On our way! Don't hold us up! Others will come after us, our brothers; you can ask them." Stop! Easy does it! Just pause a moment! Tell me where the homeland of love is, how it begins, how it ends. "Who can say? Mischievous child, love is like the wind, swift and lively, never resting. It is eternal, but not always constant. Let's go! On our way! Don't hold us up! Onward over stubble and forests and meadows! If I see your sweetheart, I'll say hello for you. My child, goodbye! Goodbye! Goodbye!"

39. *Denk' es, o Seele!* (Think of This, My Soul!)

A little fir tree is growing green somewhere in the forest, and a rose bush, who can say in what garden? They have already been chosen — think of this, my soul — to take root and grow on your grave. Two black horses are grazing in the meadow. They return home to the city cavorting merrily. They will accompany your corpse with measured steps: perhaps, perhaps even before the iron that I see gleaming on their hoofs becomes loose!

40. *Der Jäger* (The Hunter)

Three days of rain without a letup; no sunshine at this moment. For three whole days no kind word from my sweetheart's lips! She is cross with me, and I with her; that's the way she wanted it. But the sulking and the resentment gnaw away at my heart. Welcome then, pleasures of hunting, thunderstorm and rain! I button up my hot breast tightly and go to meet you jubilantly! Now she is probably sitting at home, laughing and joking with her brothers and sisters, while I hear the old leaves whispering in the forest at night. Now she is probably sitting and weeping out loud in her room with her sorrows, while I feel comfortable and secure in the darkness the way the wild animals do. No stag or doe anywhere! A shot just to pass the time! A healthy report and echo refresh the inner man. But as the thunder dies away now in the valleys all around, a sudden sorrow overcomes me, and my heart sinks all the way down. She is cross with me, and I with her; that's the way she wanted it. But the sulking and the resentment eat away at my heart. Up then, and to my sweetheart's house, and hug her around the waist! "Squeeze the rain out of my wet hair, and kiss me and have me again!"

41. *Rath einer Alten* (An Old Woman's Advice)

I was young once; I know what I'm talking about. And I've grown old, so what I say counts. Nicely ripe berries are hanging on the bush. Neighbor, in that situation, it's no help to have a fence around the garden. Merry birds know how to get there. But, my lass, let me give you some advice: keep your sweetheart in love with you, and keep him in awe of you! With two little threads twisted into one, you can pull him after you by your little finger. Being honest at heart but able to keep a secret; getting up with the sun and going to work courageously; keeping their limbs strong and their linen clean: that's what gives girls and women their value, that's what gives girls and women their value. I was young once; I know what I'm talking about. And I've grown old, so what I say counts.

42. *Erstes Liebeslied eines Mädchens* (A Girl's First Love Song)

What's in the net? Take a look! But I'm afraid! Will I grab hold of a sweet eel? Will I grab hold of a snake? Love is a blind fisherwoman. Tell your child in which direction she should reach out! It's already jumping around in my hands! Oh, sorrow! Oh, pleasure! With its twisting and turning, it is slipping onto my breast. How amazing! It's boldly biting its way right through my skin, and shooting my heart down! Oh, love, I'm scared! What should I do, what should I under-

take? The frightful thing is clicking inside of me, it's coiling itself up. I must be poisoned! It's crawling around here, digging rapturously, and it will end up by killing me!

43. *Lied eines Verliebten* (Song of a Young Man in Love)

Very early, ah, long before daybreak, my heart awakens me so I can think about you, even though healthy young men like their sleep. My eyes are awake and bright around midnight, brighter than early morning churchbells. When did you ever think about me during the day? If I were a fisherman, I would get up and carry my net down to the river; with a glad heart I would carry the fish to sell in the market. In the mill, by lamplight, the miller boy is constantly on the go, and all the machinery rattles; I would welcome that kind of energetic activity! But alas, poor fool that I am, I must idly suffer in bed, with an ill-mannered little girl on my mind!

44. *Der Feuerreiter* (The Fiery Horseman)

Do you see the red hat there at the small window again? It must be something out of the ordinary, because he's already walking up and down the room. And all at once what a crowd near the bridge, past the field! Listen! The fire bell is ringing shrilly: behind the hill, behind the hill, the mill is on fire! Look, there he is, the fiery horseman [or: the rider to fires], practically in a fury, dashing through the town gate, riding his horse that's thin as a skeleton as if he were riding a fireman's ladder! Right across country, through the smoke and heat, he is already racing, and he's at the spot! Over there it keeps on ringing: behind the hill, behind the hill, the mill is on fire! You who have so often smelled the "red rooster" from miles away, and with a splinter of the Holy Cross have sacrilegiously conjured away the flames, alas! the Enemy in the glare of Hell is grinning at you from the roofbeams. May God have mercy on your soul! Behind the hill, behind the hill, he is raging in the mill! It didn't take even an hour before the mill burst into ruins, but the bold horseman was never seen again from that time on. People and wagons in a crowd return home from all that horror; even the bell dies away: behind the hill, behind the hill. . . on fire! Some time later a miller found a skeleton, along with the hat, sitting erect against the cellar wall on the bony mare. Fiery horseman, how coolly you ride in your grave! Suddenly it all crumbles into ashes. Rest in peace, rest in peace, down there in the mill!

45. *Nixe Binsefuss* (Rushfoot, the Water Sprite)

Old Father Water Sprite's daughter dances on the ice by the light of the full moon. She sings and laughs without shyness as she passes the fisherman's house. "I am the maiden Rushfoot, and I must watch over my fish. My fish live in a chest; they eat only cold Lenten fare. The chest is of Bohemian glass, so I can count them at any time. All right, you stupid fisherman? You old fool, you can't get reconciled to the winter, can you? Let me catch you coming out with your nets! I'll rip them into shreds for you! Of course, your servant girl is pious and kind; her sweetheart is a hunter, an upright man. Therefore, as a wedding bouquet for her, I will hang a wreath of sedge outside the house and, as a present, I will give her a fish, a pike of heavy silver that goes back to King Arthur's day. It's the masterpiece of a dwarf goldsmith, and it brings its owner nothing but good luck. Year after year you can scale it, and there you have five hundred groschen in ready money. Goodbye, my child! Goodbye for today! The morning rooster is crowing in the village."

46. *Gesang Weyla's* (Weyla's Song)

You are Orplid, my land; your radiance is seen from far off. Your sunlit coast turns the water of the ocean into a mist that moistens the cheeks of the gods. Primeval waters rise rejuvenated about your hips, child! Kings, who are merely your attendants, bow before your godhead.

47. *Die Geister am Mummelsee* (The Spirits at the Mummelsee [a lake in the Black Forest long considered haunted])

Who are those coming down there from the mountain so splendidly with torches at the late midnight hour? Are they going to a dance or a feast at this time of night? Their songs sound so cheerful to me. Oh, no! Then tell me, who can they be? That which you see is a funeral procession, and that which you hear is lamentation. They are mourning for their king, the wizard, and they are bearing his pall again. Oh, woe, in that case it is the spirits of the lake! They are floating down into the Mummelsee valley. They have already stepped onto the waters of the lake. They aren't even moving or wetting their feet. They are murmuring quiet prayers like a buzz. Oh, look at the shining woman by the coffin! Now the lake is opening its green-mirrored gate. Watch out, now they are submerging! A living staircase comes swaying forth, and the hum of their songs is already coming from down below. Do you hear? Down there they are singing him to rest, down there they are singing him to rest. How beautifully the waters burn and glow! Greenish fire plays over them. The mists spook along the shore; the pond is silently condensing into a sea! Is anything going to move over there? There's a twitching movement in the middle. Oh, heaven, help! Now they are coming again, they are coming! There is an organ roar in the reeds and a clanking in the sedges. Look lively now, now is the time to run! Let's get away from here! They have scented me, they're grabbing for me, they have scented me, they're grabbing for me, they have scented me, they're grabbing for me already!

48. *Storchenbotschaft* (The Storks' Message)

The shepherd's house stands on two wheels, stands high on the heath both night and day. Many a one would like to have such fine sleeping quarters! A shepherd wouldn't change beds with the king. And even if something extraordinary should happen to him at night, he just says a prayer and goes back to sleep. A little ghost, a little witch, airy folk like that, they may knock at his door, but he doesn't answer. But one time things really got too much for him: there was a scraping at the shutter, and the dog whined. My shepherd drew the bolt, and look! there stood two storks, a male and a female. The couple made a polite bow, and would gladly have spoken, ah, if they only knew how! "What does this poultry want of me? Have you ever heard of anything like this? But I probably have a joyful message in store for me. You probably live back there on the Rhine? You've probably bitten my girlfriend in the leg? Now I suppose the baby is crying, and its mother even more, and she wishes her sweetheart were with her. And also wishes to have the baptism arranged: a little lamb, a little sausage and a little bag of money? So tell her I'll be there in two or three days, say hello to my little boy for me and stir his porridge! But wait! Why did two of you show up? I hope it isn't twins!" Then the storks rattled their beaks in the merriest key. They nodded and curtseyed and flew away, they nodded and curtseyed and flew away.

49. *Zur Warnung* (A Cautionary Tale)

Once, after a night spent in merriment, I woke up in the morning feeling strange: I was thirsty, hated the sight of water, felt funny inside, and at the same time very sentimental and softhearted, almost poetic. Yes, I asked the Muse for a song. She, with disguised pathos, made fun of me, and inspired this contemptible drivel: "A nightingale sings by the waterfall; and a bird likewise, whose name is wryneck, Johann Jakob Wryneck. He does a dance near the plants of the aforesaid waterfall." It went on in that vein; I got more and more frightened. Then I jumped up: some wine! And that's what saved me.

Take heed, you lachrymose poets: don't call upon the gods when you've got a hangover!

50. *Auftrag. Couplet* (A Commission. Comic Song)

In a poetic epistle a desperate fellow cries: "Dear Cousin, Cousin Chris! Why don't you write? You surely know that hearts that have felt the breath of love, absolutely won't stand for any fooling around, and especially when it's a poet's heart! For I am of that crew whose heads are constantly crammed; and if I am only half a poet, I am nevertheless half crazy. The god of love has placed you under an obligation to me; you know your reward in advance, and the person who reports to you will also receive something for her pains. So keep your eye open when the opportunity arises, when your sweetheart looks out of her shutter. Lure her into repeating every word that my sweetheart tells her in confidence. Then write me a twelve-sheet letter about my girl, and with that a little book of rules about how I should behave toward her, how I should behave toward her."

51. *Bei einer Trauung* (At a Wedding)

In front of witnesses who belong exclusively to the upper nobility, two of them are getting married. The organ is full of fiddles, but not the sky, I declare!* Just look, she is weeping fiercely, and he is making a repulsive face! Because you see, unfortunately, you see, love has nothing to do with the proceedings.

52. *Selbstgeständniss* (A Confession to Oneself)

I am my mother's only child, and because none of the others ever showed up—I don't know how many there would have been, six or seven—everything was reserved for me. I had to swallow love, devotion and kindness meant for a whole half dozen, and I'll never forget it as long as I live. But it might have been good for me after all if I had only gotten beatings for six.

53. *Abschied* (Farewell)

Without knocking, a gentleman comes into my room in the evening: "I have the honor to be your critic!" Immediately he picks up the candle, studies my shadow on the wall for some time, steps up close to me and backs away again: "Now, my dear young man, kindly take a look at your nose from the side like this! You must admit that it's an excrescence." "It is? Well, damn it, of course it is! Hell! I never thought, never in all my life, that I was walking around with such an enormous nose!!" The man continued talking about this and that; I swear I don't remember what. Maybe he thought I should make confession to him. Finally he stood up; I lit the way for him. When we got to the top of the stairs, I felt in a very merry mood and gave him just a little kick from behind on his seat to send him on his way. My goodness, was that a commotion, a tumbling and a stumbling! I have never seen the like; never in my life have I seen a person go down the stairs so fast!

*Refers to the expression *der Himmel hängt voller Geigen*, "things look rosy." In this case the organ is playing beautifully, but there is no rosy future for the bride and groom.

THE COMPLETE
MÖRIKE SONGS

Der Genesene an die Hoffnung.

No 1.

Hugo Wolf.

Langsam und schwer.

GESANG.

PIANO.

pp

Tödt - lich grau-te

mir der Mor-gen: doch schon lag mein Haupt, wie süss! Hoff- nung, dir _ im

Schooss ver-bor-gen, bis der Sieg ge - won - - nen hiess _

p *cresc.*

breit.

bis der Sieg _____ ge - won - nen hiess.

f *ff* *sf* *sf.* *ff*

Ped.

3

8

2

Erstes Zeitmass. *p*

O - pfer bracht' ich al - len Göt - tern, doch ver -

ges - - sen wa - rest du; seit - wärts von den ew' - gen

Ret - tern sa - hest du dem Fe - ste zu.

mit innigster Empfindung

O ver - gieb,

du Viel - ge-treu-e! Tritt aus dei-nem Däm-mer - licht, ___

dass ich dir in's e - wig neu - e, monden-hel-le An - ge-sicht einmal schau-e, recht von Herzen,

wie ein Kind und son - der Harm; ach, nur Ein - mal oh - ne Schmer-zen

schliesse mich in dei - nen Arm!

Der Knabe und das Immlein.

№ 2.

Hugo Wolf.

Mässig, zart.
(leise)

GESANG.

PIANO.

Im Wein-berg auf der Hö - he ein Häus-lein steht so win - de bang;

hat we-der Thür noch Fen - ster, die Wei - le wird ihm lang. Und ist der Tag so

schwü - le, sind all' verstummt die Vö - ge-lein, summt an der Son-nen - blu - me ein.

Imm-lein ganz al-lein. Mein

Lieb hat ei-nen Gar - ten, da steht ein hübsches Im-men-haus: kommst du da - her ge-

flo gen? schickt sie dich nach mir aus? „O nein, du fei - ner

Kna - be, es hiess mich Nie-mand Bo - ten gehn;

diess Kind weiss nichts von Lie - ben, hat dich noch kaum ge - sehn. Was

6

wüss - ten auch die Mäd - - chen, wenn sie kaum aus der Schu - le

sind! Dein herz - al - lerlieb - stes Schätz - chen

ist noch ein Mut - ter - kind. Ich bring' ihm Wachs und

Ho - nig; a - de! ich hab' ein gan - zes Pfund;

Ein Stündlein wohl vor Tag.

№ 3.

Hugo Wolf.

klag': der - weil ich die - ses sin - gen thu', herzt er ein Lieb in gu - ter Ruh', ein

Stündlein wohl vor Tag. O weh! nicht wei - ter sag'! O

still! nichts hö - ren mag! Flieg' ab, flieg' ab von mei - nem Baum! — Ach, Lieb' und Treu' ist

wie ein Traum ein Stündlein wohl vor Tag.

Jägerlied.

№ 4.

Hugo Wolf.

In die Lüf-te hoch ein Rei-her steigt, da - hin we - der Pfeil noch Ku - gel fleugt:

Tau - send-mal so hoch und so - ge-schwind die Ge - dan-ken treu - er Lie - be sind.

Der Tambour.

No 5.

Hugo Wolf.

Tscha - ko wär' ein Humpen gut, den füll' ich mit Bur - gunderblut. Und

(zurückhaltend) *(zart, etwas zögernd)*

weil es mir an Lich - te fehlt, da scheint der Mond _____ in mein Gezelt;

tempo *rit.* - - -

scheint er auch auf Fran - zösch her - ein, mir fällt doch mei - ne Lieb - ste ein: ach

tempo

weh! ach weh! ach weh! weh! ___ jetzt hat der Spass ein

Er ist's.

№ 6.

Hugo Wolf.

Sehr lebhaft, jubelnd.

GESANG.

PIANO.

Früh - ling lässt sein

blau - es Band wie - der flattern durch die Lüf - te;

sü - sse, wohl - be - kann - te Düf - te strei - fen ah -

- nungs - voll das Land.

Veil - chen träu - men

schon, _____ wol - len bal - de kom - men.

Horch, von fern _____

ein lei - ser Har - fen - ton! _____

Früh - ling, ja du bist's!

Früh - ling, ja du bist's! dich hab ich ver-

nom - men! ja du

bist's!

Das verlassene Mägdlein.

№ 7.

Hugo Wolf.

Langsam.

GESANG.

PIANO.

Früh, wann die Häh - ne krähn,

eh' die Sternlein schwinden, muss ich am Her - de stehn, muss Feu - er zün - den.

Schön ist der Flammen Schein, es springen die Fun - ken; ich schaue

so da-rein, in Leid ver - sun - ken.

etwas lebhafter — *etwas ruhiger.*

Plötz-lich, da kommt es mir, treu-lo-ser Kna-be, dass ich die

Nacht von dir ge-träu-met ha-be.

(*wie zu Anfang*)

Thrä-ne auf Thrä-ne dann stür-zet her-nie-der; so kommt der Tag her-an

o ging'er wie-der!

Begegnung.

№ 8.

Hugo Wolf.

Was doch heut Nacht ein Sturm ge-we - sen, bis erst der Mor - gen sich ge-regt!

Wie hat der un - ge-be - tne Besen Ka - min und Gas - sen aus - ge-fegt!

Da kommt ein Mäd - chen schon die Stra - ssen,

das halb ver-schüch-tert um sich sieht; wie Ro-sen, die der Wind zer-blasen, so

un-stet ihr Ge-sicht-chen glüht.

Ein schöner Bursch tritt ihr ent-ge-gen, er will ihr voll Ent-zü-cken nahn:

wie sehn sich freu-dig und ver-le-gen die un-ge-wohn-ten Schel-me an!

Er scheint zu 'fra - gen, ob das Lieb-chen die Zö - pfe schon zu - recht ge-macht,

die heu-te Nacht im off - nen Stübchen ein Sturm in Un - ord - nung ge-bracht.

Der

Bur - sche träumt noch — von den Kü - ssen, die ihm das sü - sse Kind ge-tauscht, er

steht, von An - muth hin - ge-ri - ssen, derweil sie um die E - cke rauscht.

Nimmersatte Liebe.

№ 9.

Hugo Wolf.

Sehr mässig.

ist die Lieb'! So ist die Lieb'! Mit Küssen nicht zu stil - len: wer ist der Thor und

will ein Sieb mit ei - tel Wasser fül - len? und schöpfst du an die tau - send Jahr', und

küs - sest e - wig, e - wig gar, du thust ihr nie zu Wil - len.

Fussreise.

№ 10.

Ziemlich bewegt.

Hugo Wolf.

Am frisch ge - schnittnen Wan - der - stab wenn ich in der Frü - he so durch Wäl - der zie - he, Hü - gel auf und ab: Dann,

A - dam Herbst= und Früh - lings-fie - ber, gott - be - herz - te, nie ver - scherz - te

Erst - lings= Pa - ra - di - - - ses - won - - - ne.

Al - so bist du nicht so schlimm,o

al - - - ter A - dam, wie die stren - gen Leh - rer sa - gen;

Liebst und lobst du im mer doch,

singst und prei-sest im - mer noch, wie an e - wig neu - en Schöpfungs-

ta - - gen, Dei-nen lie - - ben Schö - pfer

und ___ Er - hal - - - ter.

Möcht' es die-ser ge-ben, und mein gan-zes Le-ben wär' im leich-ten Wan-der-schweisse ei-ne sol-che Mor-gen-rei - se!

An eine Aeolsharfe.

TU SEMPER URGES FLEBILIBUS MODIS
MYSTEN ADEMPTUM: NEC TIBI VESPERO
SURGENTE DECEDUNT AMORES,
NEC RAPIDUM FUGIENTE SOLEM.
HOR.

№ 11.

Hugo Wolf.

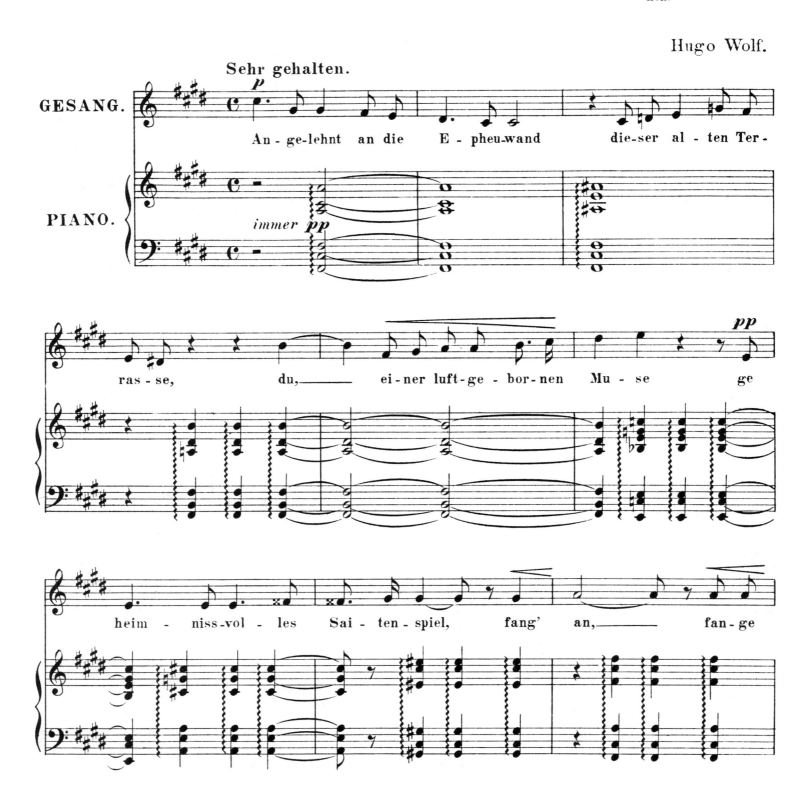

35

Früh - lings blü - then un-ter-we-ges strei - fend, ü - ber sät - tigt mit

Wohl - ge - rü - chen, wie süss, wie süss, wie

süss be-drängt ihr dies Herz!_____ wie süss be-drängt ihr dies

Herz!_____ Und säu - selt her in die Sai - ten, an - ge-

zo - gen von wohllau - tender Weh - muth,___ wach - send im Zug mei-ner

Sehn - sucht,___ und hin - ster - bend wie - der.

A - ber auf ein - mal, wie der Wind hef-ti-ger

her stösst, ein holder Schrei der Har - fe wie-derholt, mir zu süssem Er-

schrecken, meiner See - - le plötz - li-che Reg - ung;

und hier____ die vol - le Ro - se streut, ge-

etwas zurückhaltend

schüt - telt, all' ih-re Blät - ter vor mei-ne Fü - sse!

etwas zurückhaltend

Verborgenheit.

Secrecy.

№ 12.

(Slowly and with great feeling.)
Mässig und sehr innig.

Hugo Wolf.

Im Frühling.

№ 13.

Hugo Wolf.

44

der Son - - ne gold - ner Kuss mir tief bis in's Ge-blüt hin-

ein; die Au - - gen,wun - - der-bar be - rauschet,thun,

(sehr leise)
als schliefen sie 'ein,

nur noch das Ohr _____ dem Ton der Bie - ne lau - - schet.

Agnes.

№ 14.

Hugo Wolf.

Ro - sen-zeit! wie schnell vor-bei, schnell vor-bei bist du doch ge - gan-gen!

Wär mein Lieb' nur blie-ben treu, blie-ben treu, soll - te mir nicht ban - gen.

Um die Ern - te wohl - ge-muth, wohl - ge-muth

Schnit-ter-rin-nen sin - gen. A - ber, ach! mir kran-ken Blut, mir

pp

kran - ken Blut, will nichts mehr ge - lin - gen.

cresc. — — pp

Schlei - che so durch's Wie - sen-thal, so durch's Thal,

als im Traum ver - lo - ren, nach dem Berg, da tau - send-mal,

mf *f*

tau - send mal er mir Treu' ge - schwo - - ren.

O - ben auf des Hü - gels Rand, ab - ge wandt,

wein' ich bei der Lin - de; an dem Hut mein Ro - sen-band, von sei - ner Hand,

spie - let in dem Win - - - de.

Auf einer Wanderung.

№ 15.

Hugo Wolf.

schwe-ben, und ei-ne Stim-me scheint ein Nach - - ti gal len-

chor, _____ dass die Blü - then be - ben, dass die Lüf - te

le - ben, dass in hö - he-rem Roth die Ro - - sen leuch-ten vor.

Lang hielt ich stau-nend,

lust-be-klom-men.

Wie ich hinaus vor's Thor gekom-men,

ich weiss es wahr-lich sel-ber nicht.

bedeutend langsamer

Ach hier, wie liegt die Welt so licht! _____ Der Him-mel wogt in

pur-pur-nem Ge - wüh-le, rück - wärts die Stadt in gold-nem Rauch; wie rauscht der Erlen-

beschleunigend

bach, wie rauscht im Grund die Müh-le, ich bin wie trun-ken, irr -

breit

- ge-führt _____ o Mu - se, du hast

rit. 1ᵉˢ Zeitmass

mein Herz be-rührt mit ei - nem Lie - - bes - hauch!

Elfenlied.

№ 16

Hugo Wolf.

GESANG.

PIANO.

Bei Nacht im Dorf der Wäch-ter rief: El - fe! Ein

ganz kleines Elf-chen im Wal - de schlief _ wohl um die El - fe! _

Und meint, es rief ihm aus dem Thal bei sei-nem

Na-men die Nachti - gall, o - der Sil-pe-lit hätt' ihm ge - ru-fen.

Licht. „Was

sind das hel - le Fen - ster - lein? Da drin wird ei - ne Hoch - zeit sein: die

Klei - nen sit - zen bei'm Mah - le, und trei - ben's in dem

bedeutend langsamer

Saa - le. Da guck' ich wohl ein we - nig 'nein!"

Der Gärtner.
The Gardener.

N⁰ 17.

(Lightly and gracefully.)
Leicht, graziös.

Hugo Wolf.

Citronenfalter im April.

№ 18.

Hugo Wolf.

Grausame Früh-lings-son - ne, du weckst mich vor der Zeit, dem nur in Mai - en-won - ne die zar - te Kost ge - deiht!

Ist nicht ein lie - bes Mäd - chen hier, das auf der Ro - sen-lip - pe

Um Mitternacht.

№ 19.

Hugo Wolf.

Sehr ruhige Bewegung.

GESANG.

PIANO.

Ge - las - sen stieg die Nacht ___ an's Land, ___ lehnt träu - mend an der Ber - ge Wand, ___ ihr Au - ge sieht ___ die gold - ne Wa - ge nun der Zeit ___ in glei - chen Scha - len ___ stil - le ruhn; ___ und

ke - - - cker rau - schen die Quel - len her _ vor,____ sie sin - gen der Mut - ter, der

Nacht, in's Ohr____ vom Ta - - ge, vom

heu - te ge-we - se-nen Ta - - - ge. Das

ur - alt al - te Schlum - mer-lied,____ sie ach - tet's nicht, sie

ist____ es müd';____ ihr klingt des Himmels Bläu - - e sü-sser noch,____ der

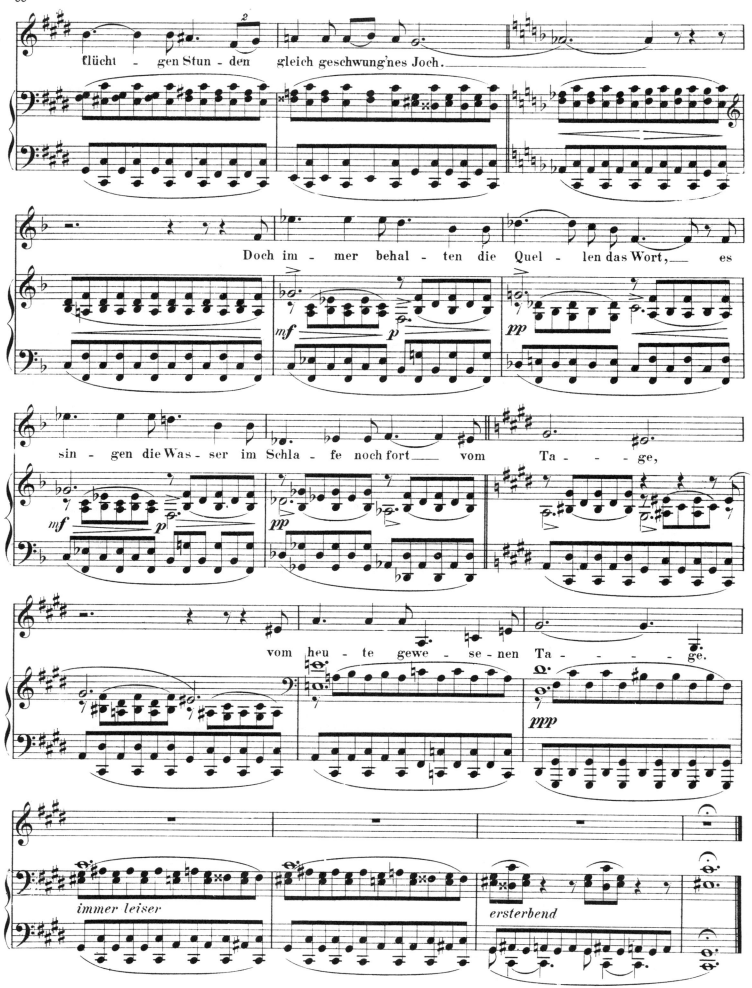

Auf eine Christblume.

№ 20.   I.

Hugo Wolf.

Toch-ter des Walds, du Li - li - en-ver - wan-dte, so lang von mir ge - such -

— te, un - be-kannte, im frem - den Kirchhof, öd' und win-ter-lich, zum er - sten

mal, o schö - ne, find'ich dich!

(leise)

Von welcher Hand gepflegt

— du hier er-blüh-test, ich weiss es nicht, noch wes - sen Grab du hü-test; ist es ein Jüng-ling,

so ge-schah ihm Heil, ist's ei - ne Jung-frau, lieb - lich fiel ihr Theil.

(immer leise)

Im nächt-'gen Hain, von Schnee-licht ü-ber-brei tet, wo fromm das Reh an dir vor-

ü - ber wei - det, bei der Ka-pel le, am krystall'nen Teich, dort sucht'ich dei-ner Hei-

Im Hauptzeitmasse.
(ausdrucksvoll)

math Zau - berreich. Schön bist du, Kind des Mon - des, nicht der Son - ne.

Dir wä-re tödt-lich and - rer Blu-men Won - ne, dich nährt, den keu-schen

Leib voll Reif_____ und Duft, himm-lischer Käl-te bal-sam sü - sse Luft.

etwas langsamer u. sehr ruhig

In dei-nes Bu-sens gold - ner Fül - le grün-

_____ det ein Wohl-ge-ruch, der sich nur kaum ver-kün-det; so duf-te-te,

be-rührt von En-gels-hand, der be-ne-dei-ten Mut - ter Braut-gewand.

pp

(zart)

Dich wür - den, mah - nend an das heil' - ge Lei - den,

p

cresc. - - -

(zart)

fünf - Pur-pur-tro-pfen schön und ein-zig klei-den: Doch kind - lich zierst du,

pp

pp

um die Weihnachtszeit, licht - grün mit ei - nem Hauch dein wei - sses Kleid.

ppp

Auf eine Christblume.

№ 21.

II.

Hugo Wolf.

Im Win - ter - bo - den schläft, ein Blu - men - keim, der

Schmet - ter - ling, der einst um Busch und Hü - gel in Früh - lings -

nächten wiegt den sammt' - nen Flü - gel; nie soll er

kos - ten dei - nen Ho - nig - seim.

Wer a - ber weiss, ob nicht sein zar - ter Geist, wenn je - de

Zier des Som - mers hin - ge - sun - ken, der - einst, von dei - nem

lei - sen Duf - te trun - ken,____ mir un - sicht - bar, dich blü - hen - de um -

kreist?____

Seufzer.

(Crux fidelis.)

Nº 22.

JESU BENIGNE!
A CUJUS IGNE
OPTO FLAGRARE
ET TE AMARE:
CUR NON FLAGRAVI?
CUR NON AMAVI
TE, JESU CHRISTE?
—O FRIGUS TRISTE!

(Aus der Passionshymne des Fortunatus.)

Hugo Wolf.

ich es he - gen, wollt' ich es pfle - gen!

Hab's nicht ge - he - get und nicht ge - pfle - get, bin todt im

Her - zen___ o Höl - len - schmer - zen!

Auf ein altes Bild.

№ 23.

Hugo Wolf.

In grü-ner Landschaft Som-mer-flor, bei küh-lem Was-ser,

Schilf und Rohr, schau,wie das Knäb-lein Sün - de-los frei

spie - let auf der Jung - frau Schooss!

Und dort im Wal - de won - ne - sam,

ach, grü - net schon des Kreu - zes Stamm!

In der Frühe.

No 24.

Hugo Wolf.

(innig und zart)

Äng - ste, quä - le dich nicht län - ger, mei - ne See - le!

Freu' dich! Schon sind da und dor - ten

Mor - gen - glo - cken wach ____ ge -

wor - - - - den.

(allmählig verklingend)

Schlafendes Jesuskind.

Gemalt von Franc. Albani.

№ 25.

Hugo Wolf.

Sehr getragen und weihevoll.

GESANG.

PIANO.

ppp

(leise)

Sohn der Jung-frau, Him - mels-kind! am Bo - den auf dem Holz der

Schmerzen ein - ge - schla - fen, das der from-me Mei-ster sinn - voll spie-lend dei - nen

leich — ten Träu-men un - ter - leg - te;

(sehr ausdrucksvoll)

Blu - me du, noch in der Knos - pe däm-mernd ein - ge-hüllt die Herr-lich-keit des

Va - ters! O wer se - hen könn-te, wel - che Bil - der hin-ter

die - ser Stir - ne, die - sen schwar-zen Wim - pern, sich in

sanf - tem Wech - sel ma - len!

Sohn der Jung-frau, Him - mels - kind.

Charwoche.

Hugo Wolf.

O Wo - che, Zeu - gin hei - li - ger Be - schwer - de!

du stimmst so ernst zu die - - ser Früh - lings - won - ne, du brei -

- test im ver - jüng - ten Strahl der Son - ne des Kreu - zes Schat - - ten auf die

lich - - te Er - de, und sen - - kest schwei - - gend dei - ne

Flö - re nie - der; der Früh - ling darf in - des - sen im - mer kei - men, das

Veil-chen duf-tet un - ter Blü-then-bäu - men und al - le Vög-lein sin - gen Ju - bel-lie - der.

O schweigt, ihr Vög - lein

auf den grü-nen Au - en! es hal - len rings die dum-pfen Glo - cken-klän - ge, die En -

-gel sin-gen lei-se Grab-ge-sän-ge; o still, ihr Vög-lein hoch im

noch etwas langsamer

Him-mel-blau-en! Ihr Veil-chen, kränzt heut kei-ne

(zart u. ausdrucksvoll)

Lo-cken-haa-re! Euch pflückt mein frommes Kind zum dunklen Strausse,

ihr wan-dert mit zum Mut-ter-got-tes-hau-se, da sollt ihr wel-ken auf des Herrn Al-ta-

Erstes Zeitmass.

re. Ach dort, von Trau-er-me-lo-die-en

trun-ken, und süss be-täubt von schwe-ren Weih-rauch-düf-ten,

sucht sie den Bräu-ti-gam in To-des-grüf-ten, und Lieb' und Früh-

-ling, Al-les ist ver-sun-ken!

Zum neuen Jahr.

KIRCHENGESANG.

№ 27.

Hugo Wolf.

hei-lig Will-kom-men, ein hei-lig Will-kom-men! Herz, jauchze du mit!

In Ihm

sei's be-gon-nen, der Mon-de und Son-nen an blau-en Ge-zel-ten des Him-mels be-

wegt. Du, Va-ter, du ra-the! len-ke du und

Erstes Zeitmass.

wen - de! Herr, dir in die Hän - de sei An -

f *p* *cresc.*

(überströmend) *ritard.*

- fang und En - de, sei Al - - - les, sei

f

a tempo

Al - - les ge - legt!

ff *p* *dolce*

dim. *pp* *rit.* *ppp*

Gebet.
Prayer.

№ 28.

Hugo Wolf.

(Smoothly.)
Getragen.

GESANG.
Voice.

PIANO.

(with devotion and fervour)
(fromm und innig)

Herr! schi-cke was du willt, ein
Lord send what Thou deem'st best _ Be

Lie-bes o-der Lei-des; ich bin ver-gnügt, dass Bei - des aus dei-nen
it or joy or griev-ing I wait Thy Will_ be-lie - - ving That both Thy

Hän - den quillt. Wol-lest mit Freu - den und wol - lest mit Lei - den mich
Love   at - test.   Not with - out   mea - sure Give   sad - ness or   plea - sure— All—

— nicht ü - ber - schüt - ten! Doch in der Mit - ten —
— mer - ci - ful Fa - ther!   For   mid - way   ra - ther—

(delicately and with expression)
(Zart und ausdruckscoll.)

doch in der Mit - ten liegt hol - des Be - schei - - den.
For   mid - way   ra - ther   Lies—   Hearts Ease' pure trea - - - sure.

An den Schlaf.

SOMNE LEVIS! QUANQUAM CERTISSIMA MORTIS IMAGO,
CONSORTEM CUPIO TE TAMEN ESSE TORI.
ALMA QUIES, OPTATA, VENI! NAM SIC SINE VITA
VIVERE, QUAM SUAVE EST, SIC SINE MORTE MORI!

MEIBOM.

№ 29.

Hugo Wolf.

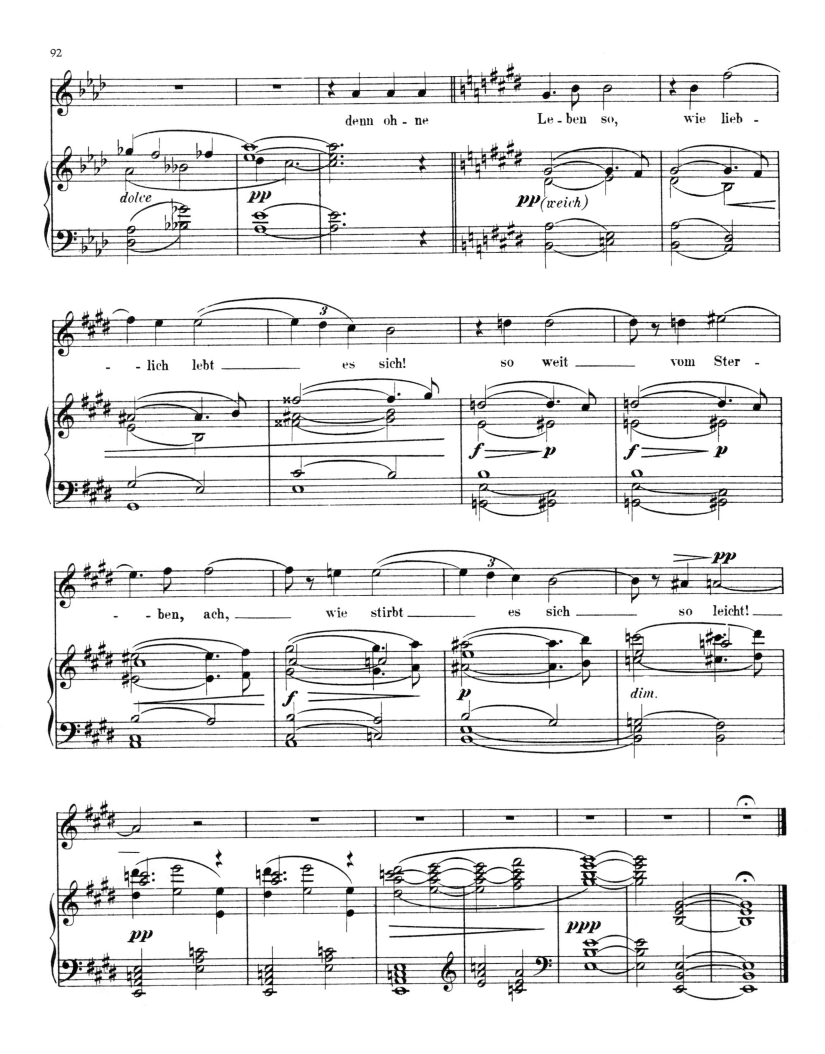

denn oh - ne Le - ben so, wie lieb -

- - lich lebt es sich! so weit vom Ster -

- - ben, ach, wie stirbt es sich so leicht!

Neue Liebe.

№ 30.

Langsam und mit der innigsten Empfindung.

Hugo Wolf.

Kann auch ein Mensch des
an - dern auf der Er - de ganz, wie er möch - te, sein?
—in lan - ger Nacht be - dacht' ich mir's, und muss - te sa - gen, nein!

95

Wo find' ich Trost.

№ 31.

Hugo Wolf.

Langsam und sehr ausdrucksvoll.

GESANG.

PIANO.

Ei - ne Lie-be kenn' ich, die ist treu, war ge - treu, so lang ich sie ge - fun - den,

hat mit tie-fem Seuf - - zen im-mer neu, stets ver-söhn - lich, sich mit mir ver-

bun - den. Wel - cher einst mit himm - li - schem Ge - dul - den

pp *f* *p* *f* *p*

bit - ter bit - tern To - des - tro - pfen trank, hing am Kreuz und

f *p* *f* *p* *f* *p*

büss - te mein Ver - schul - den, bis es in ein Meer

f *p* *f* *p*

— von Gna - de sank. *(sehr ausdrucksvoll)*

dim. *dim.* *pp*

Ar - ges Her - ze! Ja ge - steh' es nur, du hast wie - der bö -

- se Lust em - pfan - gen; from - mer Lie - be, from - mer Treu - e Spur,

ach, das ist auf lan - - ge nun ver - gan - gen.

(sehr ausdrucksvoll)

Ja, dass ist's auch, dass ich trau - rig bin, dass ich

drängend _ _ _ _ _ _ _ _ _ _ _ _ Iᵗ **Zeitmass.**

angstvoll mich am Bo - den win - de!

Hü - ter, Hü - ter, ist die

cresc. _ _ _ _ _

ff

Nacht bald hin?

Und was ret - tet mich

von Tod und Sün - de?

mf

dim.

p

ff

mf *p* *pp* *dim.* *ppp*

An die Geliebte.

№ 32.

Hugo Wolf.

Wenn ich, von dei-nem An-schaun tief ge-stillt, mich stumm

_ an dei - nem heil' - gen Werth ver-gnü - ge, dann hör' ich recht

_ die lei-sen A-them-zü - ge des En - gels, wel-cher sich in dir ver-hüllt.

Und ein er - staunt, ein fra - gend Lä - cheln quillt

(ausdrucksvoll)

(zart)

auf mei-nem Mund, ob mich kein Traum be-trü-ge, dass nun in dir, zu e - wi-ger Ge-

nü - ge, mein kühn - ster Wunsch, mein einz' - ger sich er - füllt? Von

Tie - fe dann zu Tie - fen stürzt mein Sinn, ich hö - re aus der Gott - heit nächt'ger

Fer - ne die Quel-len des Geschicks me-lo-disch rau - schen. Betäubt kehr' ich den Blick nach O -

- ben hin, zum Him-mel auf___ da lä - cheln al - le Ster - ne; ich

knie - e, ih - rem Licht ___ ge-sang zu lau - schen.

(sehr ausdrucksvoll)

(zart)

Peregrina.

(Aus: Maler Nolten.)

№ 33.

I.

Hugo Wolf.

Sehr getragen.
(innig)

GESANG.

PIANO.

Der Spie - gel die-ser treu-en, braunen Au - gen ist wie von innerm Gold ein Wie - derschein; tief aus dem Bu-sen scheint er's an - zu - sau - gen,

dort mag solch Gold in heil' - gem Gram gedeihn. In die-se Nacht des Bli -

im Tempo und Vortrag gesteigert

Peregrina.

(Aus: Maler Nolten.)

II.

Hugo Wolf.

№ 34.

Ach,   ge-stern in den hel-len Kin - der-saal, bei'm Flimmer zierlich

auf-gesteckter Ker - zen,   wo ich mein   selbst_ ver-gass   in Lärm und Scher - zen,

tratst   du,   o Bild - niss mit-leid=- schö-ner Qual;

es war   dein Geist,   er setz - te sich an's Mahl,

fremd sas - sen wir mit stumm - ver-halt'-

- nen Schmer - - - - zen; *immer beschleunigender* zuletzt brach ich

ritard.
in lau-tes Schluchzen aus, und

Erstes Zeitmass. *immer ein wenig zurückhaltend*
Hand in Hand ver - lie - ssen wir das Haus.

Frage und Antwort.

№ 35.

Hugo Wolf.

Fragst du mich, wo-her die ban-ge Lie-be mir zum Her-zen kam, und wa-rum ich ihr nicht lan - ge schon den bit-tern Sta-chel nahm? Sprich, wa-rum mit Gei-sterschnelle wohl der Wind die Flü - gel rührt, und wo-her die sü - sse Quel - le die ver-borg-nen

Was-ser führt?

(ausdrucksvoll)

Ban - ne du auf sei - ner Fähr - te mir den Wind in vol - lem Lauf!

Hal - te mit der Zau-ber-ger - te du die süs - sen Quel-len auf!

Lebe wohl.

Nº 36.

Hugo Wolf.

leich - tem Her - zen.   Le - be wohl!

(immer gesteigerter)

Ach tau - send - mal hab' ich mir es vor - ge - spro - chen;

(nachlassend)

und in nim - mer - sat - ter Qual mir das Herz da - mit ge -

bro - chen!

Heimweh.

№ 37.

Hugo Wolf.

An-ders wird die Welt mit je-dem Schritt, den ich wei - - ter von der Lieb-sten ma-che; mein Herz, das will nicht wei-ter mit.

Hier___ scheint die Son-ne kalt in's Land,___

114

giss-meinnicht! _____ Ja, die sind schön an je - dem Ort,

a - ber nicht wie dort. Fort, _____ nur

fort! Die Au - gen gehn _____ mir ü - - ber!

Lied vom Winde.

№ 38.

Hugo Wolf.

die wis - sen es nie _____ die wis - sen es nie.

Bist du klü - ger als sie, magst du es sa - gen.

— Fort, wohl auf! Halt' uns nicht auf! Kommen

an - dre nach, un - sre Brü - der, da frag' wie - der."

120

„Wer's nen-nen könn - te! Schel-mi-sches Kind, Lieb' ist wie

Wind, rasch und le-ben-dig, ru-het nie, e - wig

ist sie, aber nicht immer be-stän - dig. — Fort! Wohl-auf! halt' uns nicht

auf! _____ Fort ü-ber Stop - pel und

Wäl - der und Wie - sen! Wenn ich dein Schätzchen seh', will ich es grü - ssen.

Kind - lein, A - de! A - de!

A - de!

Denk' es, o Seele!

№ 39.

Hugo Wolf.

auf dei-nem Grab zu wur-zeln und zu wach-sen.

Zwei

schwar-ze Röss-lein wei-den auf der Wie-se, sie keh-ren heim zur

Stadt in mun-tern Sprün-gen. Sie

Der Jäger.

№ 40.

Hugo Wolf.

Drei Ta - ge Re - gen fort und fort, kein

Son - nenschein zur Stun - de; drei Ta - ge lang kein gu - tes Wort aus

mei - ner Lieb - sten Mun - de! Sie trutzt mit mir und

ich mit ihr, so hat sie's ha - ben wol - len; mir a - ber nagt's am

Her - zen hier, das Schmol-len und das Grol - - - len.

Will - kom - men denn, des Jä - gers Lust, Ge - wit - tersturm und

Re - gen! fest zu - ge-knöpft die hei - sse Brust, und jauch - zend euch ent -

ge - gen! _____ Nun sitzt sie wohl da -

heim und lacht und scherzt mit den Ge - schwi-stern; ich hö - re in des

Wal - des Nacht die al - ten Blät - ter flü - stern. Nun

etwas langsamer

sitzt sie wohl und wei - net laut im Käm - merlein, in Sor - gen; mir

p (Zart und ausdrucksroll)

dim.

1⁵ Zeitmass.

ist es wie dem Wil - de traut in Fin - ster-niss ge - bor - gen.

pp

kein Hirsch und Reh - lein ü - ber - all! Ein Schuss zum Zeitver-

trei - be! Ge-sun-der Knall und Wie-der-hall er-

frischt das Mark im Lei-be. —

Doch wie der Don-ner nun ver - hallt in Thä-lern, durch die Run - de,

Grol - - len. Und auf! und nach der

Lieb - sten Haus! und sie ge - fasst um's Mie - der! „Drück' mir die nas-sen

Lo-cken aus, und küss' und hab' mich wie-der!" *(sehr schnell und leidenschaftlich)*

Rath einer Alten.

Hugo Wolf.

Bin jung ge - we - sen, kann auch mit re - den, und alt ge - wor - den, drum gilt mein Wort.

Schön rei - fe Bee - ren am Bäum - chen han - gen: Nach - bar, da hilft kein Zaun um den

Gar - ten; lu - sti - ge Vö - gel wis - sen den Weg.

etwas langsamer

A - ber, mein Dirn - chen, du lass dir ra - then: hal - te dein

Schätz - chen wohl in der Lie - be, wohl in Re - spekt!

Mit den zwei Fäd - lein in Eins ge - dre - het,

poco rit.

ziehst du am Klei - nen Fin - ger ihn nach.

Auf - rich - tig Her - ze, doch schwei - gen

kön - nen, früh mit der Son - ne mu - thig zur Ar - beit,

ge - sun - de Glie - der, sau - be - re Lin - nen.

Erstes Liebeslied eines Mädchens.

№ 42.

Hugo Wolf.

1ˢ Zeitmass.

Haut,_____ schiesst's Her-ze hin - un - - ter! o Lie - -

be, mir graut!_____ Was thun,

was be - gin-nen? Das schau-ri - ge Ding, es schnal-zet da -

drinnen, es legt sich im Ring._____ Gift ___ muss ich

ha - ben! Hier schleicht es he - rum, thut won -

ein wenig zurückhaltend - - - *tempo*

- nig-lich gra - - ben und bringt mich noch um!

Lied eines Verliebten.

№ 43.

Hugo Wolf.

In al-ler Früh, ach, lang vor Tag, weckt mich mein Herz, an dich zu

den - ken, da doch ge - sun - de Ju - gend schla - fen mag.

Hell ist mein Aug' um Mit - ter - nacht,

hel - ler als frü - he Mor - gen - glo - cken: wann hätt'st du

je am Ta - ge mein ge - dacht?

Wär' ich ein Fi - scher, stünd' ich auf, trü - ge mein Netz hin -

ab ___ zum Flu - sse, trüg' herz - lich froh die Fi - sche

zum Ver - kauf. ___ In der Müh - le, bei

Licht, der Müh - ler - knecht tum - melt sich, al - le Gän - ge klap - pern;

Kopf.

Der Feuerreiter.

№ 44.

Hugo Wolf.

Und auf ein - mal welch Ge-

wüh - le bei der Brü - cke, nach dem Feld!

immer *ff*

Horch! das Feu - er - glöck - lein gellt:_____

(*wild*)

hinter'm Berg, hinter'm Berg brennt es in der Müh - le!

fff

Schaut! da sprengt er wü - thend schier durch das

Thor, der Feu - - - er - rei - ter. auf dem

rip-pen - dürren Thier, als auf ei - ner Feu - - er - lei - ter!

Quer - feld - ein! durch Qualm und Schwü - le rennt er schon, und ist am

zunehmend

fre - ventlich die Gluth bespro-chen — weh! dir grinst vom Dach - ge-stüh - le

dort der Feind im Höl - len-schein. Gna - de Gott der See - le dein!

più f   *ff*

I. Zeitmass.   (wild)

hinter'm Berg,   hinter'm Berg

fff

rast er in der Müh - le!

Kei - ne
Stun - de hielt es an, bis die Müh - le borst in Trüm - mer;
doch den ke - cken Rei - ters-mann sah — man von der Stun - de nim - mer.

152

153

Nixe Binsefuss.

№ 45.

Hugo Wolf.

vor - - bei.

Dieselbe Bewegung.

„Ich bin die Jungfer Bin - sefuss,   und

mei-ne Fisch' wohl hü - ten muss,   mei-ne Fisch' die sind im Kas-ten, sie

ha - ben kal - te Fas - ten; von Böh - mer - glas mein Kas - ten ist, da zähl' ich sie zu

je - der Frist. _____ Gelt,

Fi - schermatz? gelt, al - ter Tropf, dir will der Win - ter nicht in Kopf?

Komm mir mit dei - nen Ne - tzen! die will ich schön zer - fe - tzen!

Dein Mägd-lein zwar ist

fromm und gut, ihr Schatz ein braves Jä - gerblut. Drum häng' ich ihr, zum

Hoch-zeitsstrauss, ein schil - fen Kränz-lein vor das Haus, und ei - nen Hecht, von

Sil - ber schwer, er stammt von Kö - nig Ar - tus her, ein

Zwer - gen = Goldschmids = Mei - sterstück, wer's hat, dem bringt es ei - tel Glück: er

lässt sich schuppen Jahr für Jahr, da sind's fünfhun-dert Grösch - lein baar.

Wie zu Anfang.

A -

de, mein Kind! A - de für heut!

Der Mor - gen-hahn im Dor - fe schreit."

Gesang Weyla's.

Weyla's Song.

№ 46.

Hugo Wolf.

Die Geister am Mummelsee.

Hugo Wolf.

Vom Ber-ge was kommt dort um Mit-ter-nacht spät mit

Fa-ckeln so präch-tig her - un - ter? Ob das wohl zum Tan - ze, zum Fe - ste noch geht? Mir

klin-gen die Lie - der so mun-ter. O nein! so sa-ge, was mag es wohl sein? Das,

was du da sie - hest, ist Tod-ten-ge-leit, und was du da hö - rest, sind Kla - gen. Dem

Kö - nig, dem Zau -be -rer, gilt es zu Leid, sie brin -gen ihn wie -der ge - tra - gen. O weh! so

nissvoll)

sind es die Gei -ster vom See! Sie schweben her -un -ter in's Mummel-see-thal __ sie

etwas zurückhaltend

ha -ben die See schon be -tre -ten __ sie rüh -ren und ne -tzen den Fuss nicht ein -mal __ sie

schwirren in lei -sen Ge -be -ten __ o schau' am Sar-ge die glän -zen-de Frau! Jetzt

PP (Das Motiv im Basse markirt)

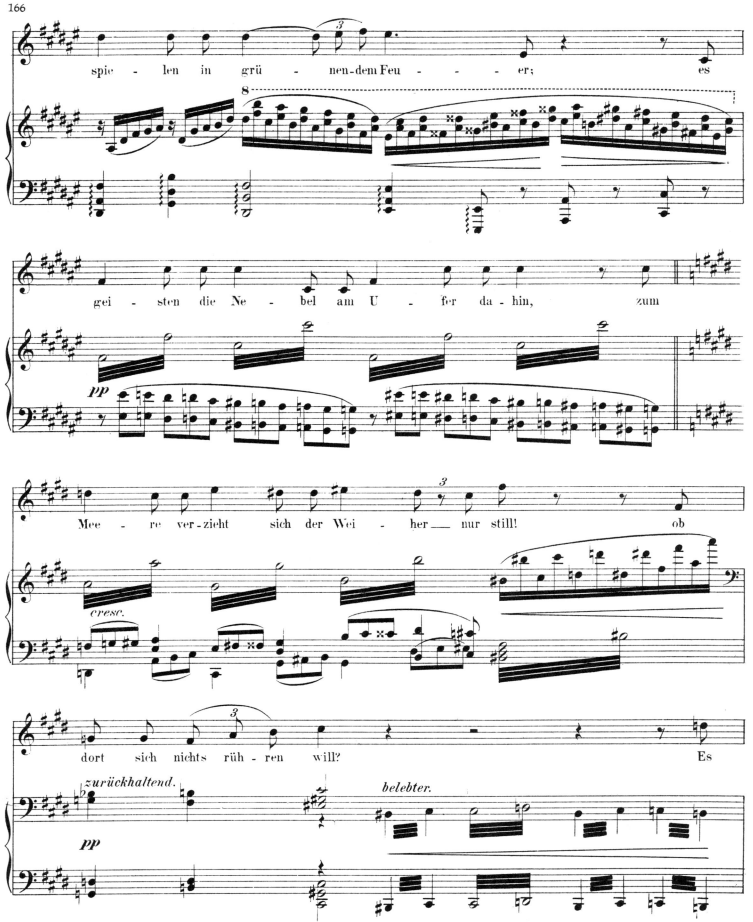

zuckt in der Mit-ten __ o Him-mel! ach hilf! nun kom-men sie wie-der, sie kom - men! es

or - gelt im Rohr und es klir-ret im Schilf; nur hur-tig, die Flucht nur genommen! Da-von! sie

wit-tern, sie haschen, sie wit-tern, sie haschen, sie wit-tern, sie haschen mich schon!

Storchenbotschaft.

№ 48.

Hugo Wolf.

Gemächlich.

GESANG.

PIANO.

Des Schä-fers sein Haus und das steht auf zwei Rad, steht hoch auf der Hei-den, so frü-he, wie spat; und wenn nur ein Man-cher so'n Nacht-quar-tier hätt'! Ein Schä-fer tauscht nicht mit dem Kö-nig sein Bett. Und käm' ihm zur Nacht auch was Selt-sa-mes vor, er be-tet sein Sprü-chel und legt sich auf's Ohr; ein

Geistlein, ein Hex-lein, so luf-ti-ge Wicht', sie klo-pfen ihm wohl, doch er ant-wor-tet nicht.

Ein-

mal doch, da ward es ihm wirklich zu bunt: es knopert am La-den, es winselt der Hund; nun

zie-het mein Schäfer den Rie-gel— ei schau! da stehen zwei Störche, der Mann und die Frau.

I. Zeitmass.

Das Pär-chen, es ma-chet ein schön Com-pli-ment, es

rit. *f*

möch-te gern re-den, ach, wenn es nur könnt'! Was will mir das Zie-fer?_ ist so was er-hört? Doch

lebhaft

rit.

ist mir wohl fröh-li-che Bot-schaft be-schert.

wieder langsamer

bewegter

rit.

p stacc.

Ihr seid wohl da-hin-ten zu Hau-se am Rhein? Ihr

lebhaft

stacc.

sehr gedehnt

lebhaft

wer-den doch, hoff'ich, nicht Zwillin-ge sein?_ da klappern die Stör-che im lus-tig-sten Ton, sie

nik_ken und kni_xen und flie-gen da-von _ sie nik_ken und kni_xen und

flie-_gen da-von._____

Zur Warnung.

№ 49.

Hugo Wolf.

war ich am Morgen seltsam auf gewacht:

Durst,

Was-serscheu, ungleich Geblüt; da-bei gerührt und weichlich im Gemüth, beinah po-e-tisch,

ja, ich bat die Mu - se um ein Lied. Sie, mit verstelltem Pa-thos, spot - tet'mein,

gab mir den schnö - den Ba - fel ein:

Lebhaft, (phantastisch)

„Es schlagt ei - ne Nach-ti-gall ____ am Was-ser-fall; und ein Vo - gel e - benfalls, der schreibt sich Wen - de - hals, Jo-hann Ja - kob Wen-de-hals; der thut tan - zen bei den Pflan - zen ob be-meld - ten Was-ser-falls —".

(grell)

so ging es fort; mir wur - de im-mer bän - ger.

Jetzt sprang ich auf: zum Wein!

Der war denn auch mein Retter. ___ Merkt's euch, ihr

thränen-rei-chen Sän - ger, im Kat - zen-jammer ruft man kei - ne Göt-ter!

Auftrag.
(COUPLET.)

№ 50.

Hugo Wolf.

In po- e - ti-scher E - pi-stel ruft ein des-pe - ra-ter Wicht: lie - ber Vet - ter! Vet -ter Chri-stel! Wa - rum schreibt Er a - ber nicht? weiss Er doch, es las - sen Her - zen, die die Lie - be an - ge-weht, ganz und

gar nicht mit sich scher - zen, und nun vol - lends ein Po - et!

Denn ich bin von dem Ge - li -chter, dem der

Kopf be - stän dig voll; bin ich auch nur halb ein Dich - ter, bin ich

doch zur Hälf-te toll.

A - mor

hat Ihn mir ver-pflich-tet, sei - nen Lohn weiss Er vor - aus, und der

Mund, der Ihm be-rich-tet, geht da - bei auch leer nicht aus.

Pass' Er denn zur gu-ten Stun-de, wenn Sein Schatz durch's Lädchen schaut, lock' ihr

poco rit.

je des Wort vom Mun - de, das mein Schätz-chen ihr ver-traut.

Schreib' Er mir dann von dem Mäd-chen ein halb Dut-zend Bo-gen voll, und da-

ne - ben ein Trac - tät - chen, wie ich mich ver - hal - ten soll,

wie ich mich ver - hal - ten soll.

Bei einer Trauung.

№ 51.

Hugo Wolf.

Seht doch, sie weint ja gräu-lich, er macht ein Gesicht ab-

scheu-lich! _____ Denn lei-der frei - lich, frei - lich

kei - ne Lieb' ist nicht da - bei.

Selbstgeständniss.

№ 52.

Hugo Wolf.

Ich bin mei-ner Mutter ein - zig Kind.

und weil die an-dern aus - blie-ben sind, was weiss ich wieviel, die

Sechs o - der Sie-ben, ist e-ben Al - les an mir hängen blieben;

ich hab' müssen die Lie - be, die

Treu - e, die Gü - te für ein ganz halb Du - tzend al - lein auf - es - sen,

ich will's mein Lebtag nicht ver - ges - sen. Es hät - te mir a - ber noch wohl

mö - gen from - men, hätt' ich nur auch Schläg' für Sech - se be - kom - men.

Abschied.

Hugo Wolf.

№ 53.

fern:

„Nun, lie-ber jun-ger Mann, sehn Sie doch ge-fäl-ligst 'mal Ih-re Nas' so von der Sei-te an!

Sie ge-ben zu, _____ dass das ein Auswuchs is:"

_ Das? Al-le Wet-ter _ ge-wiss!

Ei

rasch die Trepp' hin-ab - gehn!